MAKE IT!

Miniature Robots

Anastasia Suen

Rourke
Educational Media
rourkeeducationalmedia.com

SUPPLIES TO COMPLETE ALL PROJECTS:

- 3-volt motor (with wire leads)
- 9-volt battery
- 9-volt battery clip (with wire leads)
- AA battery
- bamboo skewers (2)
- binder clips (1 ¼ inch or 31.75 millimeters wide) (4 medium)
- binder clips (3/4 inch or 19 millimeters wide) (2 small)
- books (4 for ramp)
- cardboard
- coil cell battery (with wire leads)
- coin
- DC motor with shaft (small)
- double-sided mounting tape
- hex nut (small)
- hot glue
- on/off switch (SPST)
- paperclips
- plastic bottle caps (4)
- plastic straws (2)
- Plasticine or Play-Doh
- pliers (for bending)
- pliers (for cutting)
- round plastic container
- rubber band (wide)
- ruler
- scissors
- stick-on eyes
- table
- tape (wide)
- thin marker pens (4)
- toothbrush bristle head
- vibrating disk motor (with wire leads)
- wire stripper
- wooden dowel (5/16 inch or 8 millimeters diameter, 12 inches or 30 centimeters length)

Table of Contents

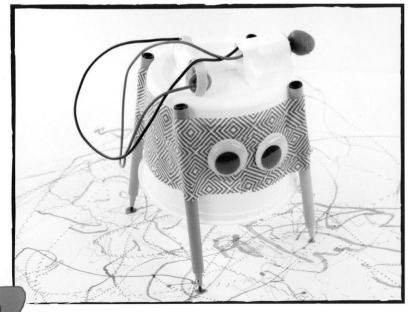

Miniature Robots

You can make these miniature robots with school supplies, recycled materials, small batteries, and motors.

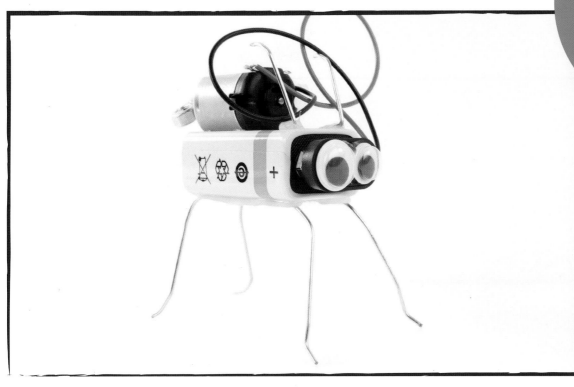

Make your own miniature robots! Build a robot that walks downhill without a motor. Turn a toothbrush into a brushbot. Use a hex nut to make a robot bug wiggle. Transform a recycled container into an art robot. Wire a single pole **switch** to power a tiny robot car.

Robot Walker

- wooden dowel (5/16 inch or 8 millimeters diameter, 12 inches or 30 centimeters length)

- 4 medium binder clips (1 ¼ inch or 31.75 millimeters wide)

- 2 small binder clips (3/4 inch or 19 millimeters wide)

- 4 books (for ramp)

- flat table

MAKE A WALKING ROBOT!

Here's How:

1. Pull up the silver clip wings so they touch both the sides of all six clips.

2. Slide the wings of a medium clip onto the dowel. Repeat with another medium clip. Then slide both medium clips to the center of the dowel.

3. Hold a small clip by the wings. Press down to open the small clip.

4. Close the small clip on the dowel next to a medium clip. Repeat with another small clip on the other side.

5. The small clips will keep the medium clips at the center of the dowel.

Tip: The silver wings on these clips will swing back and forth. These are the walker's legs. The flat parts of the clips are the walker's feet. Place the wings of the small clips forward so they do not touch the feet as they swing back and forth.

6. Hold a medium clip by the wings. Press down to open the medium clip.

7. Then close the medium clip on the dowel next to end. Close the clip so the silver wings extend down. Repeat with another medium clip.

8. Make a walking ramp with two books. Place two books on the table for the base. Place two books at an angle to make a ramp.

9. Move the walker to the top of the ramp with the arms facing forward. Tap one end of the dowel and let go. The robot will walk down the ramp.

Tip: Tapping one end of the dowel will lift one of the robot's feet in the air. Then **gravity** will take over and the robot will start walking downhill. This passive dynamic walker robot does not need a motor. When you place this robot at the top of a shallow incline, gravity will make it move.

Longer Legs

Now that you know how it works, make a walking robot with longer legs. You can make a tiny robot walker with a bamboo skewer, beads, cardboard, craft sticks, and glue.

You can make a larger walker with Tinkertoys. Use rods, circles, connectors, and spools to make the hips and legs. Then add a long rod and a spool to each foot so the walker extends beyond the ramp. If you want to use this project as a science experiment, add more weight to the end of the long rods and record how that changes the robot's movement.

Brushbot

YOU WILL NEED:

- coil cell battery (with wire leads)

- vibrating disk motor (with wire leads)

- wire stripper

- toothbrush bristle head

- pliers (for cutting)

- double-sided mounting tape

- scissors

- stick-on eyes (2)

- flat table

Tip:
Ask an adult to cut the handle off the toothbrush with cutting pliers.

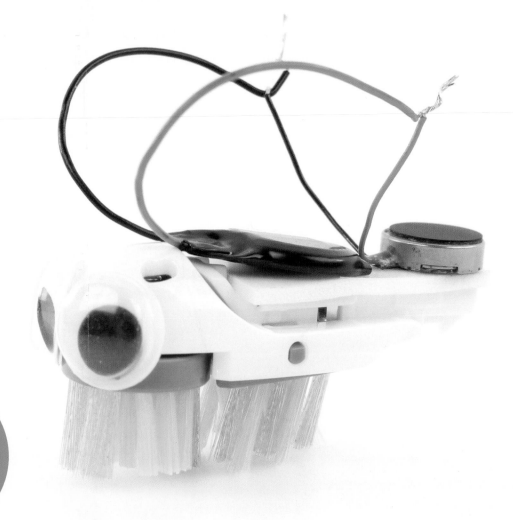

CREATE A BRUSHBOT FROM A TOOTHBRUSH!

Here's How:

1. Make the robot wider by spreading out the toothbrush bristles with your fingers.

2. Use the wire stripper to uncover 1/4 inch (6 millimeters) of wire on all four wire leads.

3. Line up the **battery** and the motor next to the brush. Turn them around so that the wires all point to the top of the brush, not the handle. Turn the motor over as needed to keep both of the red wires on the same side of the brush.

4. Cut a small square piece of mounting tape to fit under the motor. Peel the backing off one side. Stick the tape on the motor. Then peel off the backing on the other side. Place the motor at the front edge of the toothbrush head.

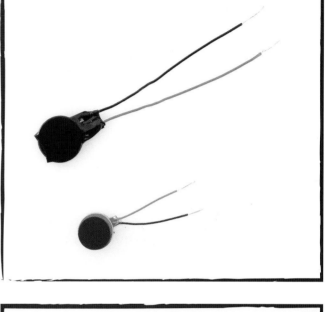

Tip:
Do not tape the wires to the toothbrush head. Place the motor on the end of the toothbrush with the red and black wires facing forward.

5. Cut another small square piece of mounting tape to fit under the cell battery.

6. Peel the backing off one side of the tape. Stick the tape under the battery. Then peel off the backing on the other side.

7. Place the cell battery on the toothbrush head behind the motor. The wires will stick up in the middle of the brush.

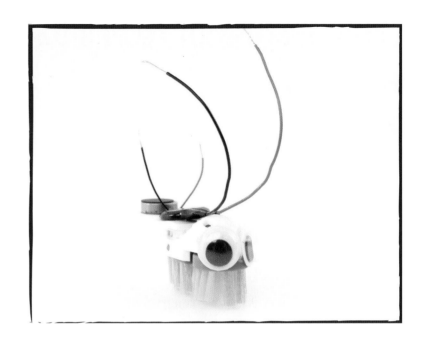

8. Add the stick-on eyes to the front of the brush. Place one on each side.

9. Pull both red wires up. These are the positive wires. Twist the two red wires together to begin making your **circuit**.

10. The two black wires are the negative wires. When you twist both black wires together, you close the circuit. Now the robot will start moving. To stop your robot, untwist the black wires to open the circuit.

Tip: Electricity flows from negative to positive. Build your circuit in the opposite direction. Connect the positive wires first. Then connect the negative wires. The electricity will flow from the battery to the motor on the black wires. Then the electricity will flow back from the motor to the battery on the red wires.

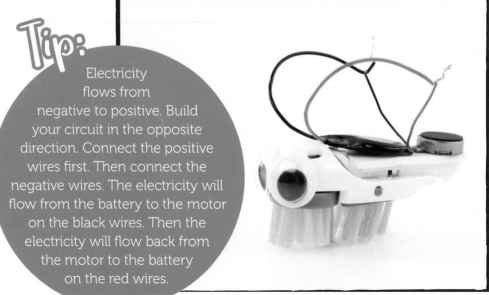

Bendy Legs

Give your robot legs by adding chenille stems. Bend the stems across the middle of the brush. Two stems will give your robot four legs. Add another stem to try six legs. If you use four stems, your robot will have eight legs like a tarantula! Will you give it eight eyes, too?

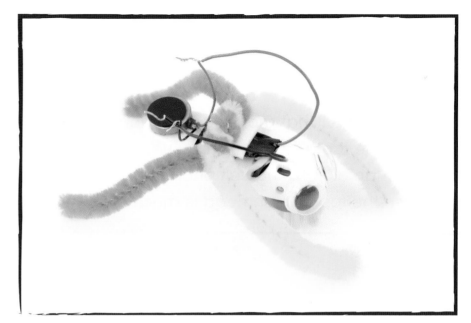

Tip:

You can use this robot for a science experiment by predicting and then recording how it moves when you add more legs or bend the legs in new directions.

13

Why Does It Work?

When the motor vibrates, it makes the robot move. This small button motor is the same motor that makes a cell phone vibrate. The toothbrush head moves farther than a vibrating cell phone does because the toothbrush head is much lighter.

Some cell phones have a motor shaped like a cylinder. The motor has a shaft that spins. A half-circle weight is attached to a bolt placed on the shaft. As the shaft spins, the half-circle weight spins, too. Because the weight on the shaft is not symmetrical, it throws off the motor's balance. That makes the motor move back and forth. This movement makes the cell phone vibrate.

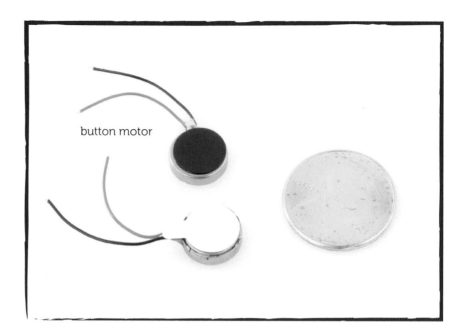

button motor

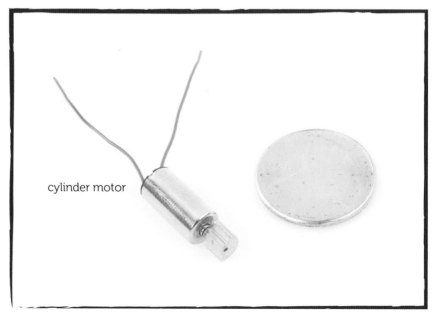

cylinder motor

Robot Bug

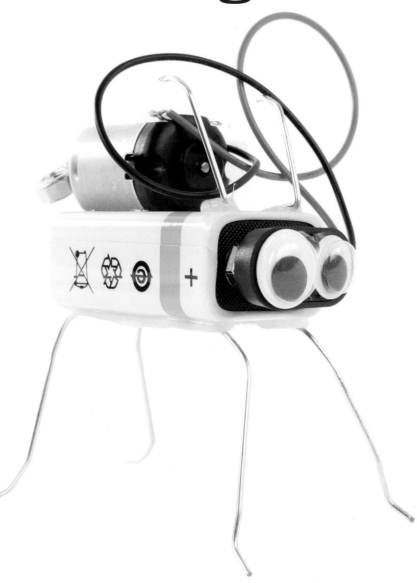

YOU WILL NEED:

- 9-volt battery
- 9-volt battery clip (with wire leads)
- wire stripper (if needed)
- small DC motor with shaft
- small hex nut
- hot glue
- paperclips
- pliers (for bending)
- pliers (for cutting)
- stick-on eyes (2)

Tip:

A hex nut is a hexagonal nut. It has six flat sides.

USE A HEX NUT TO MAKE YOUR OWN VIBRATING MOTOR!

Here's How:

1. Add hot glue to one side of the motor shaft.

2. Hold the bolt so the hole in the middle faces you. Then place one of the bolt's flat sides on the hot glue.

Tip:

Ask an adult to help with you with the hot glue.

3. Add hot glue to one wide, flat side of the motor. Turn the motor over so the glue faces down.

4. Hold the bottom of the 9-**volt** battery with your other hand.

5. Place the glued side of the motor on the lower half of the wide, flat side of the battery.

Tip!

Make sure that the motor shaft extends beyond the end of the battery.

6. Connect the wire leads on the battery clip to the motor. Use the wire stripper to uncover the wire leads as needed. Pull a wire to each metal tab and push it down through the opening. Twist each wire around the metal tab.

7. After you connect the wires, plug in the battery clip to test the circuit. If the circuit is closed, the bolt on the shaft will spin.

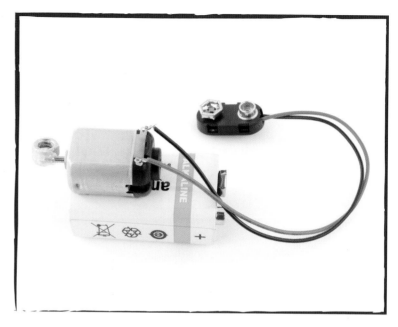

8. Unplug the battery clip for now. Bend the paperclips into legs and antennae. Use pliers as needed to cut or bend the clips. Then use hot glue to attach the metal legs and antennae to the battery.

9. Add the stick-on eyes. Put them on the side of the battery or the bottom of the battery clip. Then plug in the battery clip and watch your robot bug move!

Tip! If the shaking moves the wires and opens the circuit, the robot will stop moving. If that happens to your robot, ask an adult to add a drop of hot glue to hold the wires on the motor tabs.

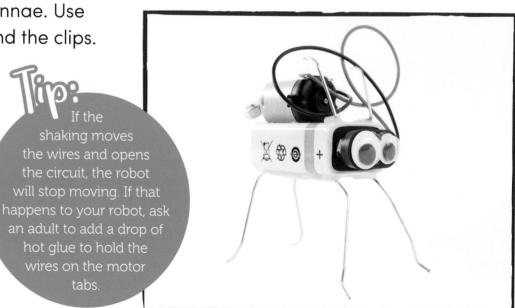

Add Wood

If you use wood to make the robot's legs and antennae, you can paint them with fun insect colors. Try toothpicks, bamboo skewers, or craft sticks. After the paint dries, use hot glue to attach the wood to the battery. You may decide to glue the antennae to the bottom of the battery clip. Remember to stick on the eyes so your robot bug can see where it is going.

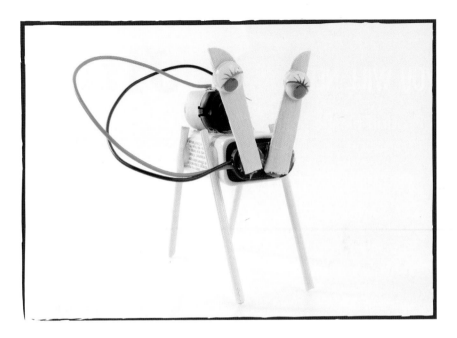

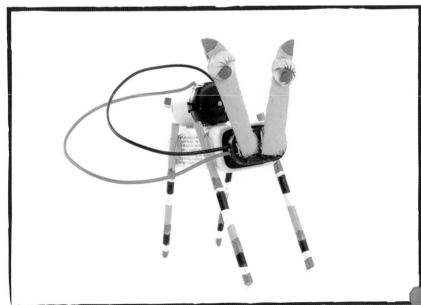

Jitterbug Art-Bot

YOU WILL NEED:

- round plastic container

- thin marker pens (4)

- AA battery

- 3-volt motor (with wire leads)

- wire stripper (if needed)

- wide rubber band

- scissors

- wide tape

- stick-on eyes (2)

- Plasticine or Play-Doh

MAKE A RECYCLED ART ROBOT!

Here's How:

1. Recycle a round plastic container. After you wash it and dry it, place it on a flat table. This is the robot body.

2. Tape the four thin marking pens to the cup as robot legs. Make sure that the top of the pens stick up in the air above the edge of the cup. Leave the pen caps on for now.

3. Turn the robot over so it stands on all four legs. Give the art robot a face by adding the stick-on eyes.

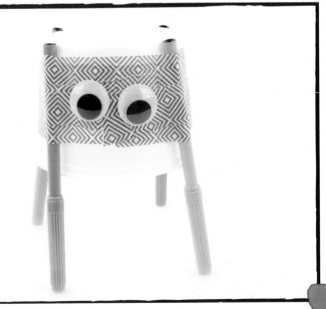

Tip:

Space the four legs evenly so the robot will stand up when you turn it over.

4. Use the wire stripper to uncover the wire leads as needed.

5. Make the DC motor into a vibrating motor by adding an uneven weight to the shaft. Try a small ball with Play-Doh or Plasticine. Roll the ball into an egg shape. Press the shaft into the small side of the egg-shaped clay.

6. Place the motor on top of the robot. Tape it down near the edge of the container so the shaft spins without hitting the side of the container.

Tip:
Test the AA battery. Connect a wire from the motor to each end of the battery. If the motor does not spin, replace the battery.

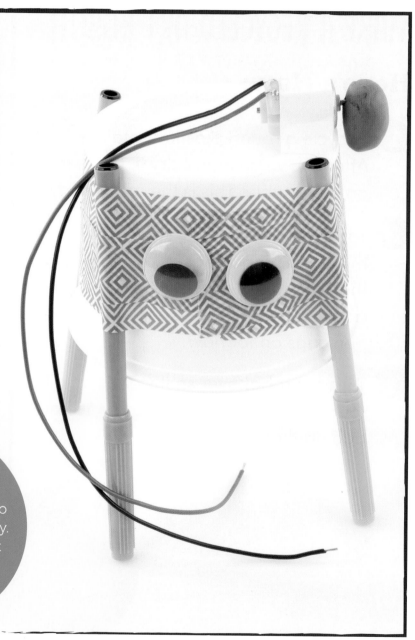

7. Wrap a wide rubber band around the battery. Then tape the rubber band wrapped battery onto the top of the robot. Place it behind the motor. Tuck the red wire inside the rubber band.

8. Take off the pen caps and place the robot on a big sheet of paper.

9. Tuck the black wire inside the rubber band to start the robot. Pull the black wire out to stop the robot.

Tip!

If the rubber band is too long to hold the wires tightly, cut it shorter and tape it down. The wide rubber band should hold the red and black wires to the positive and negative contacts on each end of the battery.

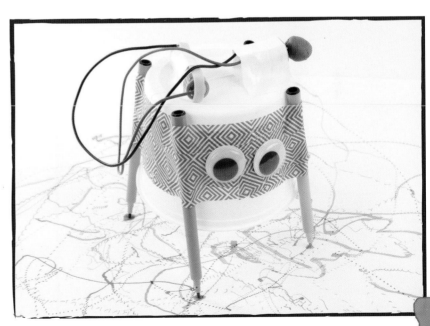

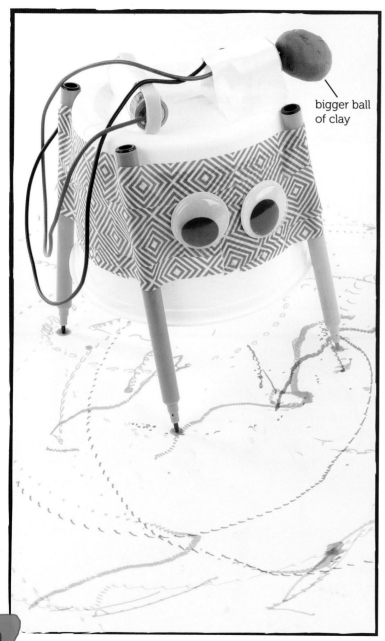

bigger ball of clay

Variations

You can use your art-bot for a science fair project by changing the weight on the motor. Make a prediction first. How will changing the shape or the location of the weight affect how the robot moves? The drawing that the art-bot makes will show the results.

Test one change at a time. Change the shape of the Plasticine. Or move the weight and press the motor shaft into a different part of the shape.

For a really big change, move the motor to the center of the bot. Tape it so the motor shaft points up and spins the weight like a helicopter. Center the weight so it is evenly balanced and see if the bot moves. Then move the weight more and more off-center.

Use a new sheet of paper each time you change or move the weight. After you release the black wire to stop the art-bot, log that change in a notebook or on the drawing. Record your progress step by step.

Rolling Robot Car

YOU WILL NEED:

- 9-volt battery
- 9-volt battery clip (with wire leads)
- wire stripper (if needed)
- small DC motor with shaft
- on/off switch (SPST)
- scissors
- plastic straws (2)
- cardboard
- coin
- ruler
- hot glue
- plastic bottle caps (4)
- bamboo skewers (2)
- pliers (for cutting)
- rubber band

USE A SWITCH TO TURN A TINY ROBOT CAR ON AND OFF!

Here's How:

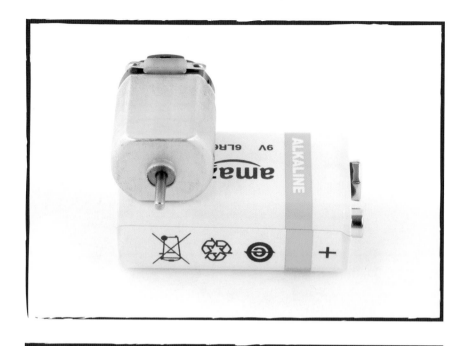

1. Begin with the robot body. Add a line of hot glue to the lower half of the battery. Place the motor on the glue. Make sure that the motor shaft extends beyond the edge of the battery.

2. Use a ruler to measure the width of the battery. Cut two lengths of plastic straw that are 1/4 inch (6 millimeters) longer than the battery on each side. These straws will hold the axle to the body later.

Tip:

Ask an adult to help you with the hot glue and the cutting pliers as needed.

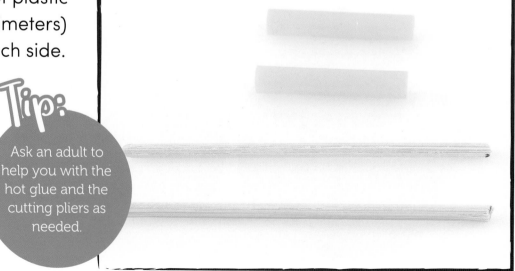

3. Make two axles. Measure 3 inches (7.62 millimeters) on each bamboo skewer and cut to size.

4. Trace the four plastic caps on the cardboard. Then trace a small coin inside each cardboard circle to make a smaller circle. Cut out the smaller circle.

5. Slide the short straw on each wooden axle. Then slide a cardboard washer on each end of the straw. Glue the cardboard washers to the skewer at the ends of the straw.

6. Place one end of the wooden axle into a plastic cap. Add hot glue inside the cap to hold the skewer in place. Repeat until all four wheels are secured.

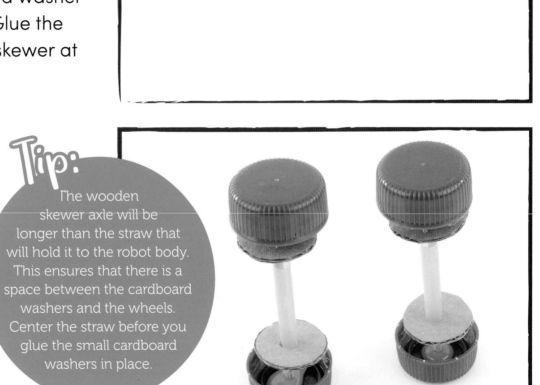

Tip:
The wooden skewer axle will be longer than the straw that will hold it to the robot body. This ensures that there is a space between the cardboard washers and the wheels. Center the straw before you glue the small cardboard washers in place.

7. Snap the battery clip onto the battery. Pull the wires back to the motor. Cut the black wire so it is just long enough to reach the front tab on the motor.

8. Use the wire stripper to uncover the wire leads in the black wire. Then wrap the short black wire from the battery clip to one tab on the on-off switch. Wrap the long black wire around the other tab on the on-off switch.

on-off switch

9. Glue the on-off switch to the side of the motor.

10. Connect the loose long black wire to a tab on the motor.

11. Cut the red wire so it only reaches the second tab on the motor. Use the wire stripper to uncover the wires. Then connect the red wire to the motor tab.

Tip: You can use a dab of hot glue to hold each wire to the tab. Glue the wires to the tabs on the switch before you attach the switch to the motor. After you wrap the remaining wires to the motor tabs, you can add a dab of hot glue to those tabs too.

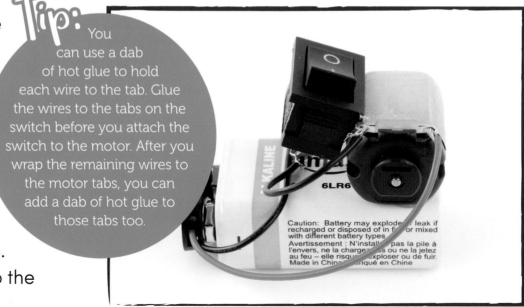

12. Turn your robot car over and glue the straws on each axle to the body.

13. Place a rubber band on the motor shaft. Then pull it around the rear axle between the washer and the wheel.

14. Put your robot car wheels on the ground and press down the switch. Watch your little robot car go!

Why Does It Work?

This simplest on-off switch has one input **terminal** and one output terminal. The input terminal is called the pole. The output terminal is called the throw. This simple switch has a single pole and a single throw. It is an SPST switch.

After you connected all of the wires, your robot car did not start moving until you turned the switch on. When the switch is turned off, the circuit is still open. Electricity cannot flow through an open circuit.

When you turn the switch on, the circuit closes. Now the electricity can flow through the circuit and make your robot move.

ON-OFF SWITCH

input terminal   output terminal

Glossary

battery (BAT-uh-ree): a container filled with chemicals that produces electric power

circuit (SUR-kit): a complete path that electricity can flow through

gravity (GRAV-uh-tee): the force that pulls things down toward the surface of the Earth

switch (SWICH): the piece of electrical equipment that turns an electronic item on or off

terminal (TUR-muh-nuhl): the entry or exit point of a component in an electric circuit

volt (VOHLT): a unit for measuring the force of an electric current

Index

Show What You Know

1. How can a robot walk downhill without a motor?

2. Why does a circuit need both red and black wires?

3. What happens when there is more weight on one side of the motor shaft?

4. Why does the rubber band on the art-bot need to be a tight fit?

5. Is the circuit in the SPST switch diagram open or closed? Explain your reasoning.

Further Reading

O'Hearn, Michael, *Awesome Space Robots*, Capstone Press, 2013.

Shulman, Mark, *TIME For Kids Explorers: Robots*, Time For Kids, 2014.

Swanson, Jennifer, *National Geographic Kids Everything Robotics: All the Photos, Facts, and Fun to Make You Race for Robots*, National Geographic Children's Books, 2016.

About the Author

Anastasia Suen is the author of more than 300 books for young readers, including *Wired* (A Chicago Public Library Best of the Best Book) about how electricity flows from the power plant to your house. She reads, writes, and edits books in her studio in Northern California.

Meet The Author!
www.meetREMauthors.com

www.rourkeeducationalmedia.com

PHOTO CREDITS: Cover, Back Cover, Pages 1, 4, 5, 6, 7, 8, 9, 10, 11, 12, 13, 14, 15, 16, 17, 18, 19, 20, 21, 22, 23, 24, 25, 26, 27, 28, 29: © creativelytara; Page 13 (tarantula): © Okea; Page 19 (locust): © THEGIFT777

Edited by: Keli Sipperley
Cover and Interior design by: Tara Raymo • CreativelyTara • www.creativelytara.com

Library of Congress PCN Data

Miniature Robots / Anastasia Suen
 (Make It!)
 ISBN 978-1-64156-444-1 (hard cover)
 ISBN 978-1-64156-570-7 (soft cover)
 ISBN 978-1-64156-689-6 (e-Book)
Library of Congress Control Number: 2018930472

Rourke Educational Media
Printed in the United States of America,
North Mankato, Minnesota